Don't Get Fooled Again

An Insider's Guide to the 7 Questions You MUST Ask to Avoid Hiring the Wrong Real Estate Agent (Again)

Aaron Hendon | Christine & Company

Aaron Hendon | Christine & Company
Copyright © 2016 Aaron Hendon
All rights reserved
ISBN-13: 978-1533589866
ISBN-10:1533589860

CONTENTS

Acknowledgements

Among the thousands of people I could acknowledge for helping make this book possible, two stand out head and shoulders above the rest:

Kael Balizer, my best friend, love of my life, my wife and the world's greatest mother, who mostly tolerates me working 24/7 and is only interested in me having it all.

Christine Robertson, my team leader, mentor, business partner and work wife, who listens to me as bigger than I know myself to be.

Introduction

I'm sorry.

I know we don't know each other, and we've probably never met, but given you are reading this book there's a high likelihood that you had a home to sell and it didn't sell.

You went through all that hassle, all that trouble, all that expense, and now what? You still have the house and all the plans you had are on hold.

Why were you selling? Did you want to downsize to live in a home that makes more sense for your situation? Were you moving some place larger so the kids can get their own room (and you can have your own bathroom)? Did you need to sell to be closer to work? School? A better neighborhood?

And now what? You're left holding the bag, confused as to what really happened. Why didn't your house sell? Everyone around you seems to be selling theirs – what's different about you?

And all you hear from your realtor, if you hear anything at all, is that you need to lower the price.

That is maddening.

I understand your frustration and I appreciate your willingness to even read this book. I bet you don't think all that highly of my profession at this point.

And I don't blame you.

In fact, it's for that reason I wrote this book. Because all real estate agents are not created equal. Like any other profession, there are good ones and bad ones (it's just that the bar to entry is so low in real estate that it tends to have a lot of bad ones).

I realize that it's not without reason Realtors, in general, have a less than spectacular reputation.

Honestly, if the fact that the ones that are just not very good at their job wasn't such a massive advantage to the clients *I represent*, I'd feel bad for the clients *they represent*.

To be perfectly clear – I don't ever recall dealing with a dishonest Realtor. I also rarely deal with a Realtor that is unpleasant, rude or unhelpful. The industry does tend to attract those at least mildly interested in customer service so there is some sort of base line there.

At the same time a surprising number (to me anyway) of Realtors seem to me to be playing some game other than "sell my clients' home for the most money, in the least amount of time, with the least hassle".

Some simply don't have any distinctions in delivering extraordinary service.

Some don't seem to care very much about anything other than getting the transaction closed so they can move on to the next one.

This all adds up to make a really bad situation for the consumer.

Look at it this way:

1. Realtors, for the most part, seem to be helpful and pleasant.

2. Most people don't really know how the game is played.

    Therefore:

3. What people are left with is choosing a Realtor based solely on either a gut feeling they have when they meet, or the advice of a friend or family member, or they read a bunch of reviews online from complete

strangers and then move forward with someone and hope for the best.

Well, that my friends, is pretty crazy.

Let's step back for moment and think this through.

Buying or selling a home is, in almost all cases, the single largest transaction anybody will ever make.

You're talking about entering into a deal that entails hundreds of thousands of your dollars, something that will undoubtedly touch virtually every aspect of your life, every day, for the foreseeable future.

On top of that, this is a transaction that's not only complicated but also something that most people do maybe three times during their entire lives.

And so for a transaction that is complex, life changing and *THE MOST EXPENSIVE THING YOU WILL EVER SELL,* you are about to do it based solely on the recommendation of a coworker?

You're willing to trust that to your mother's best friend's husband?

You're going to put that deal in the hands of that lady you met at your school auction because you have a good feeling about her?

You're afraid it'll be awkward if you don't use your kid's soccer coach?

Or worse, you are going to apply the same rules you use to buy something on Amazon or pick a restaurant on Yelp and look for someone who has the best online reviews and/or the cheapest price?

Stop it.

This is why over half the Realtors I work with are just plain mediocre – **because there is nobody vetting them based on their actual performance!**

Why? Why aren't consumers vetting their performance? Why don't consumers do any real due diligence?

Don't you think that's interesting? I sure do.

I'm particularly fascinated by it because determining the likelihood that a particular Realtor is going to deliver above average performance is so simple.

Now, it's not foolproof, but there are some surefire, telltale signs that separate an above average Realtor from a mediocre one.

Success leaves a track record.

In fact, with just a simple interview anyone can feel confident that they've found the right person to represent them in this, large, complex and singularly impactful transaction.

The biggest hurdle you faced when you selected your last Realtor was it didn't look to you like you were actually hiring someone to work for you.

Why do I say that?

Because if you thought you were hiring someone to work for you, you would interview them, because that is just what people do when they are hiring someone to work for them and **almost nobody really interviews prospective Realtors.**

Look, if you are trying to make friends (or not alienate friends) then go ahead and hire your kid's soccer coach.

If what matters to you is the way you might look to the people in your book club if you didn't use Agent Jane to sell your home, then go ahead and hire Agent Jane.

And if what matters most to you is getting the most amount of money for your home, in the least amount of time, with the least hassle, then maybe you should make sure the person you hire is the best at getting the most money in the least amount of time with the least hassle.

Wouldn't it be smart to ensure that the person you hire could demonstrate that they produce the results you are looking for?

Shouldn't they be both competent and trustworthy?

And since you will be spending a bit of time with them, shouldn't they be someone you enjoy spending time with and someone who's communication style works for you?

And you do know how people find someone with all those qualities, don't you?

They interview them.

You should plan on doing this in the same way you would interview anyone for any job that involves hundreds of thousands of your dollars - because this one does!

At the end of the day, I think people know they should do this. I also think they don't because they don't know what to ask, so, rather than risk looking foolish, they just skip the interview.

Most people would rather chew their arm off than risk looking foolish.

I understand this. It's why I won't ask for directions.

But we are talking about *real money here.* So the answer isn't don't interview people.

That's a mistake that I see cost people tens of thousands of dollars every day, and is the reason I am writing this guide.

Now, in real estate I realize that there often is what's known as an asymmetry of information. One side knows way more about the process than the other.

The process of home buying or selling, for better or worse, is not transparent and it is complex.

I highly recommend you spend a lot of time learning what you can on any number of useful websites.

But I don't care how much information you get from Web MD, if you believe that makes you a doctor, you're a fool. And if you pretend that Redfin or Zillow make you a Realtor, you'll soon discover the truth behind the adage that a fool and their money are soon parted.

That said, the amount of information available on the internet can help you immensely in this process and the more educated you become the better. That's the real purpose of this guide.

I want to provide you with a framework of questions that will guide you to finding the best possible person to represent you.

After reading this, feel free to add any other questions you think are important. The key is to handle it like a professional interview.

Think of all the normal things you consider when interviewing someone.

- Were they on time?

- Did they treat you with respect (or were they condescending)?

- Were they prepared?

- Were you left smarter for having spoken with them (or were you left confused)?

- Did they handle this like they were applying to run your business?

9

- Is this someone you'd like to spend time with?

Using the seven questions that follow as a framework when interviewing everyone applying for the position of representing you will leave you clear and confident that you've made the best choice.

I want this to give you a way to compare apples to apples. To quantify people's results in a way that clearly shows their track record of success in the areas you care most about.

If you care about time and money, and how to get more of it, then use these questions.

If you care about not making waves or not offending people, you don't need this.

Be clear, doing this will make you distinctly different.

Many Realtors will balk when asked these questions.

I say that's a good thing as it weeds out the ones that aren't going to get it done that much faster.

Realtors are used to selling themselves on their charisma and online reviews. They are shockingly unprepared to account for their own performance.

If at any time you have questions or would like to talk about anything in this guide, feel free to call or email me.

All the best to you in your next real estate transaction.

Aaron Hendon
Cell: 206-280-3312
Email: aaron@ChristineAndCompanyHomes.com

Question 1

How many transactions did you do last year? How many so far this year?

OK. I know that's two questions. And they make sense to ask at the same time so I added them together. Sue me.

Did you know that the average Realtor does five transactions per year? At a median price of $219,000 (the median price in the US as of this writing) the average Realtor makes about $33,000 in gross commissions annually.

That doesn't seem like enough to live on and should beg the question: do you really want to hire someone who does real estate part time, or has another job or worse, whose business is failing?

I recommend you find someone who does at least 15-20 transactions a year. If they work with a team, (and that's even better for reasons I'll get into later) make sure their team is doing about 15 per agent.

Less than that and I would start to wonder why? What's wrong with the way they do business that they can't do at least a couple of deals every month?

Clearly someone doing less than a deal every month is doing this as a hobby and not a profession. They should be thanked for their time and you should move on. Let them learn on someone else.

This is also when I'd find out how long they've been in the business. Someone in business for 5 years that's doing 20 transactions might not be as on the ball as someone just starting out that did 17 their first year.

As for how many so far this year, you are out to determine if their business is growing or contracting.

In other words, if they said they did 30 transactions last year, and its October now, and they've only done 10 so far, clearly they're not online to match, or increase, last year's production and you should find out "why?"

Asking "why do you think that is?" gives them a chance to talk and you a chance to learn more about how they communicate.

Anyone who makes you feel stupid for asking should be sent packing.

The answer to this question will not only give you insight into their business but the market as a whole.

If the market is strong and their business isn't growing, I'd be concerned that maybe they have something else going on in their life that's taking precedence over their business.

Conversely, if the market is weak and their business is growing, I'd be more confident that they are doing something right.

Question 2

How much of your business is referral or repeat business?

Business models matter.

Why?

Because many agents get their business by attracting "leads" through on and offline marketing efforts. They often use call centers and fast paced scripts and dialogues to "capture" new business.

Relying solely on this business model could mean that they are not organized to take care of you after the sale. They tend to look at the sale of your home as a single, discrete transaction, one of many, in a long line of transactions.

Someone who does more than half their business from referrals and repeat business tends to look at the sale of your home as the beginning of a lifelong relationship.

They are likely to have structures and systems set up to take care of you before, during and after the sale.

Their business is designed to deliver such an extraordinary level of service and produce results so far above average that their past clients come back and tell their friends.

For this reason alone someone who does 100 transactions a year may not be better than someone who does 20. If the 20 are all from past clients that would use that Realtor again and the 100 are all from internet leads bought from Zillow, who would you trust more?

Question 3

Do you have a team or are you solo?

Hiring someone on a team, or that runs a team, is preferable.

The number one complaint I hear from people about their last agent was that they didn't communicate enough or that they somehow felt that their agent didn't have time for them.

You already know I'm recommending you hire someone who's busy. I think you should want to find someone doing a lot of business, and unless they have a team you run the risk that they won't have time for you.

Ask them who their team consists of. This varies widely and there's not just one way this is supposed to look.

What you want to know is that they have both the office staff to handle the paperwork and logistics of the transaction as well as other trained agents who can communicate and work with you should your agent not be available.

Find out if the person you are interviewing will be working with you personally every step or do they have specialists to handle various aspects of the transaction. There are advantages and disadvantages either way, and the important thing is you are comfortable with how they do it.

Find out if they have vacations planned during your transaction. I've closed deals for clients while on vacation so, again, no "right" answer.

Find out if they have hours or days they don't work. Some people don't work after 6:00 P.M. or on Sundays. Is that OK with you?

Some people like their employees to be available nights and weekends and some people are less demanding.

You'll need to make this call and decide what works for you and your needs. The point here is that you are informed and can make a decision that works for you.

Question 4

What is your commission?

Ah, the question about money.

This is your chance to check on their negotiation skills. Industry standard is a 6% commission which is split 3% for the buyer's agent and 3% for the listing agent.

Discount brokerages offer, surprise, a discount.

While I'd find it difficult to believe that you like a bargain more than I do, there are certain things I don't search for bargains on.

I don't really want a discount defense attorney (I've never needed one, it's just an example ☺). If someone in my family, heaven forbid, needed a medical specialist, I also wouldn't shop based on price.

Think about what the offer of a discount really means.

Discounts anywhere in business **ALWAYS** mean one of two things.

1. They are planning on making it up on volume. Think Costco and Amazon. They have lower overhead, they sell in bulk, they use their lower price to attract a larger volume of customers and their smaller profit margin is compensated by a larger number of sales.

2. The product, offering or service, is of lower value and the market will not pay full price for it. Look at it this way: if the market felt their service was worth more, wouldn't they be charging more?

That's it. It's one of those two things.

They're not offering a discount because they're nice.

They're either going to try to make it up on volume or the market has determined they are worth less money. **That's not a real estate thing - that's a business thing – a consumerism thing.**

This means you need to ask yourself if you're OK with being part of that "volume" or if you're ok with a lower quality agent.

You also need to keep in mind that a big piece, perhaps the largest piece, of the value a good Realtor provides is their ability to negotiate the best possible price for you. This is quantifiable (as you'll see later) and asking this question will allow you to see how well they negotiate.

Consider that how they negotiate with you is a direct indicator of how they will negotiate for you.

If they cannot negotiate well with you for their fee, what are the odds they will negotiate well to defend your equity?

Think about it. If you're an average home owner, you don't buy and sell very many homes, especially not compared to a professional Realtor.

So here you are, someone with very little background in real estate negotiations and you have just moved your Realtor from 3% down to 2.5% commission. You probably feel pretty good about that.

What you're missing is that the Realtor you are working with just got out negotiated by you, someone with virtually no experience, while trying to defend their own money!

How quickly are they going to fold when faced with a professional Realtor when you're counting on them defending your money?

Talk about pennywise and pound foolish!

BTW - this is why every full service Realtor I know loves negotiating against a discount Realtor. They tend to be younger and less experienced – and they have already told the world they can't even negotiate their own price (because if they could get full price for their services, wouldn't they?)

It's almost always their plan to work on volume, which means they're not focused on building a long term relationship. They'd just as soon spend a few more of your dollars, get the deal done, and move on. Yay for my clients!

Discount Brokerages don't make sense to me as business model, but, as a full service Realtor, I'm obviously biased.

This is just another piece you'll need to decide for yourself.

Question 5

Relative to the current market, tell me about your performance last year?

This is the real money question.

The answer will tell you two things.

1. Do they know, and can they communicate, the current market conditions as they pertain to you? Are they speaking in a way that actually communicates to you? This is so important. How they explain this is critical to you as there are so many details throughout the transaction and this question can help you determine if they're competent at communicating to YOU.

   Do they make sure you understand what they are saying, or are they rushed, unsure and confused? Do they make you feel smart for asking and are you actually smarter (more informed) for having asked?

2. More importantly, you will learn about their actual performance. If you're looking to buy, they should be able to show you that they've negotiated prices below market average. If you are selling, they should be able to show you they get more than market average.

If their performance isn't better than average, you'll need some other really good reason to hire them.

This is so basic that it shocks me people don't ask this. How could you ever trust that you were getting the best possible deal without seeing both what is actually happening in the market and how a particular agent performs in that market?

Remember – this is your business. You are hiring someone to run your business. Your business is worth hundreds of thousands of your dollars. Please make sure you get someone who is competent in handling businesses like yours.

More than anything else they say during an interview, these numbers are their "track record". It's what you can use to gauge how effectively they do their job.

While past performance doesn't guarantee future performance, and every home presents a unique situation, if you're expecting a Realtor whose past performance is below average to suddenly get you more money for your home than average, you need to think again.

NOTE: It is possible (maybe even likely) the Realtor you are interviewing might not know this information off hand.

On one hand this is forgivable as we've already established that they are almost never asked for it so why would they have it?

At the same time – you gotta think: "Why should someone have to ask them for their performance before they'd bother to go find out what it is? What have they been using to measure their performance?"

Most Realtors know how many transactions they've done and the dollar volume of those transactions. This is the measure of the size of their personal business, what they count on in their pocket. That's nice – if you're them! That's how they did for themselves – not how well they did for their clients.

That they know one number and not the other says a lot about where they focus their attention – their own business vs. their clients'.

Question 6

Can I have three or four references to call, please?

The trick here is you need to call them.

Call their references.

Seriously, pick up the phone and call them.

If the Realtor you're interviewing came to you via a trusted source, fine, maybe you don't need to call anyone else. That's your choice.

But if this is a Realtor that you're getting off the internet or some other source, you'd do well to speak to people that have used them previously.

When you call ask their previous client how much over (for a sale) or under (for a buy) the deal was and how many days it was on market.

Ask if anything didn't work or didn't go well.

Ask if there is anything they wish went differently with their transaction.

Online reviews are fine but actually speaking to someone that worked with them is always better. First of all, it's one thing to ask a client to write an online review, and it's another to ask if they are willing to take calls from other prospective clients.

An agent that has clients they can give you to call is already light years ahead of someone who just wants you to read online testimonials.

Question 7

At what price would you list my home and what do you think it will sell for?

Most importantly, ask them to show you the evidence that supports their price. Make them show you comparable properties (comps in real estate jargon) and local market statistics.

Never choose an agent simply because they say they'll sell your home for the highest price – unless, of course, they're buying it themselves.

Make sure the evidence they present makes sense to you. Selling your house is YOUR business - make sure you can own their recommendations.

The most appropriate way to look at the value of your home is to look from the perspective of a buyer – based on what's available in the market right now, how much would you pay for your home?

This is where your own due diligence can pay off – are the comparable homes they show you homes that you've seen? Are they bringing new information to the table? Does the information make sense? Are they making a cogent, sensible case for their price?

If you're a buyer, obviously this question doesn't make sense. Instead, you can ask, "Given what I'm looking for (this includes location and size of home) how long should it take you to find something that will work for me?"

If you're a buyer, and you can afford to wait to buy, I recommend you ask "What's the best time of year for me to be shopping in my area?" They should be able to provide you with historical trends that show the seasonality of the market and when you're more likely to find the best deals.

In all cases you are looking for someone who is going to be straight with you and who is demonstrating having your best interests at heart.

Are they interested in you buying or selling now even though the seasonal trends would indicate waiting is better? Do they even know the seasonal tendencies and how they impact buyers vs. sellers?

They need to know because you need to know because, after all, it is your business.

Conclusion

Whether you are buying or selling, the way the Realtor answers these questions is almost as important as the actual answers.

While these questions and their answers will help you determine which real estate agent is right for you, the best rule of thumb is to continue to ask questions until you're comfortable with the situation and the person.

Like I said before – almost nobody ever does this kind of interview. Don't be surprised if the Realtor you talk to has never seen anything like this.

Be aware that they might not be prepared with all this information at their fingertips as nobody has ever asked them for it.

While someone who does have this information ready and available might be a better choice, it's probably worth giving someone a day or two to pull together what they need.

No matter what, in no case should you be made to feel stupid or over protective or annoying or like a pest for asking these questions.

Anybody who feels like they don't have the time to answer these is unlikely to understand what it means to have a fiduciary interest in you and should be politely dismissed from consideration.

Remember, you're looking to hire a business partner. If they don't express partnership with you, why would you hire them?

As for us, are there questions I've missed? Do you still have questions? Please let me know. I'd love to hear from you. As always, I am available and at your service.

About Me

My favorite job of all time has always been waiting tables. I loved it. Waiting tables is just pure service. Nothing to think about except how to best take care of these guests, and to this day, I just love when I get a waiter that really gets that whole idea.

It's so simple that I'm surprised it's so rare to find waiters that really get it.

To me, real estate is just like that. Pure service.

Nothing to do but take total care of these people right in front of me. It's from there that I developed these four pillars for my business.

I. **Educate** – Real estate is historically not very transparent. There are a lot of moving parts and they have big ramifications. The first part of my service is to make sure my clients understand everything that could, is and will happen. I am certified to lead the First Time Home Buyer Programs for the state of Washington and always start my consultations with discovering how much my clients already know and how I might best fill in the blanks.

They are the ones that are going to live with the consequences of my actions and making sure they are confident every step is paramount to me.

II. **Advocate** – Having someone on your side the whole time is critical. Someone who is fighting for your best interests. Someone who demonstrates fulfilling the fiduciary interest they are obliged to deliver.

What could be more important than trusting that the person representing you has taken all the actions (especially the ones you'll never know about) that made sure you got the best possible deal? From initial consultation to closing and beyond, my team and I are there, making sure my clients have everything they need, every step of the way.

III. **Negotiate** – The heart of negotiation is creating win-win deals. Knowing what a win for each side looks like, and then developing and executing an effective strategy to get both sides a win, is the key.

And good negotiators leave a track record of extraordinary performance behind. They have their clients pay less, and earn more, than negotiators who are less skilled – and they do so in a way that leaves everyone with the experience of having gotten what they wanted. I don't win unless my clients do and my track record speaks for itself.

IV. **Communicate** – On one level my commitment to communication is simply that 7 days a week you'll always get a returned call (or text, or email, depending on your preference) within 3 hours. You'll never be in a situation where you have a want, or a question, or a need, and not be able to have it answered quickly.

Additionally, having spent over 20 years in training for active and perceptive listening I am clear that communication takes place not in speaking but in carefully listening to what my clients need (we were given two ears but only one mouth for a reason ☺). This is the final pillar upon which I have built my business.

Thanks for reading this and if at any time you think I might be of service, please do let me know.

Feel free to call me at 206-280-3312 or email me at aaron@christineandcompanyhomes.com